NATURAL TREASURES

field guide for kids

written and illustrated by

Elizabeth
Biesiot

Denver Museum of Natural History
and
Roberts Rinehart Publishers

For my children,
Meryl and Corey,
who share their treasures with me.
—E.B.

Supported in part by the
Lloyd David and Carlye Cannon Wattis
Foundation

International Standard Book Number
1-57098-082-9
Library of Congress Number 96-067088

Published in cooperation with the
Denver Museum of Natural History
by Roberts Rinehart Publishers
5455 Spine Road, Boulder, Colorado 80301

Published in the UK and in Ireland by
Roberts Rinehart Publishers
Trinity House, Charleston Road,
Dublin 6, Ireland

Distributed in the U.S. and Canada by
Publishers Group West

Printed in Hong Kong

Project Manager: Betsy R. Armstrong
Designer: Ann W. Douden
Editor: Alice Levine
Proofreader: Lori Kranz

Illustrations on pages 44-45 and 62-63 have been redrawn
from *A Field Guide to Mammal Tracking in North America*
by James Halfpenny, illustrated by Elizabeth Biesiot, with
permission from Johnson Books, Boulder, CO.

clues all around us

Look at, listen to, smell, and examine your world every day. When you do, you'll notice clues that can tell you about the animals that live in our yards and in parks, meadows, fields, and forests. A clue may be something you see—like feathers or chewed twigs. It may be a sound—a sharp chirp or a steady buzz. It may be a smell—pleasant or not so pleasant. The clues in this book are like pieces of puzzles that are put together to make pictures of the animals that live alongside you.

In this book you will find illustrations, descriptions, and clues. The pictures and descriptions will help you identify the animal clues that are all around you. Some clues might occur throughout the year; but others occur only in certain seasons. Before you begin to explore, be sure to match the section of the book with the season of the year you are experiencing: spring, summer, fall, or winter. Remember, use all your senses. As you become familiar with the clues around you, match them to the animals in the book. If you come across words you don't understand, look in the glossary.

a clue directory

Think about the different kinds of clues that would help identify animals.

Sight clues: Look—and be careful where you step.

Look for tracks.

Tracks indicate if an animal is moving slowly or quickly. If the tracks are close together, the animal is moving slowly. If they are far apart, the animal is moving quickly.

Tracks show the direction the animal was traveling. In which direction do the claws point?

Look for droppings.

👁 Look at the size and shape of the droppings to see how big the animal is.

👁 Some animals use droppings to indicate their territory.

👁 Droppings can tell you what an animal has been eating. Look at droppings to see if they contain bits of bone, feathers, or fur, or plant fiber or seeds.

Look for homes.

👁 Nests, burrows, and dens are types of animal homes.

👁 Flattened grass might have been a bed where an animal rested.

Look for territory marks on trees.

👁 Antler rub marks could indicate deer or elk territory.

👁 Claw marks could mark territory or could have been made by climbing animals.

👂 **Sound clues:** Listen—and be tuned in to what you hear.

Listen for the voices of animals.

👂 Cries may warn other animals that you are in the area.

👂 Calls are often to a mate.

👂 The cry of a young animal tells the parents it needs to be fed.

Listen for sounds of movement.

👂 Buzzing lets you know an insect is passing by.

👂 The sounds of leaves crunching, gravel moving, and water splashing tell you an animal is trying to hide or is hunting.

👃 **Smell clues:** Take deep breaths—and be aware of unusual odors.

Smell territory markers.

👃 Animals mark their territory by scratching their droppings to release the odor.

👃 The odor of urine sprayed on bushes and tree trunks is a smell marker.

👃 When an animal rubs against bushes, trees, and posts, the scent it emits lets others know that it has been around.

Smell the animal's odor.

👃 Some animals spray an offensive odor to protect themselves from being eaten.

Some animals smell and taste bad when they are captured or injured by a predator. The predator might think again about eating another animal that looks like the one that was so unpleasant.

Evidence clues: Observe—and think about what the animal left behind.

Find animal body coverings.
Bits of fur, feathers, skin, insect wings, and shell are exciting clues.
As insects, reptiles, and other animals grow, they leave behind old skin or outside shells they have outgrown.

Check out the clues and identify the animals.
You may be familiar with many of the animals or clues in this book. Others you may never have seen. The clues help you learn more about familiar animals and also help you identify new animals. With practice you will become a good nature detective!

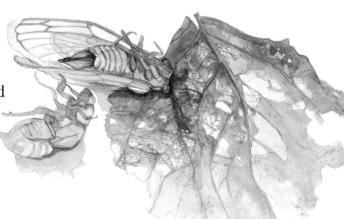

Find evidence of eating.
Nibbled leaves and nutshells indicate an animal that eats plants.
Pieces of bone, fur, and feathers may indicate an animal that eats meat.

SPRING

in springtime

In springtime,
the air and the earth
begin to warm up. You will see
more animals than you did in the
winter. You will find clues that indicate
animals are feeding, growing, mating,
making a home, and producing young.

A nest of young cottontail rabbits is hidden below the
protective branches of a bushy evergreen. This shelter
provides the perfect place for a rabbit warren.

clues

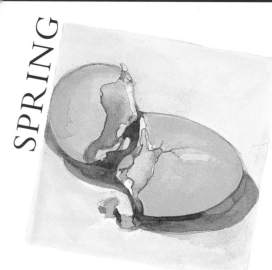

👁 In spring, look at shrubs and trees for nests lined with mud.

✋ Look for pieces of blue eggshell in lawns.

🎵 Listen for the male bird's spring song: *cheer-up*.

✋ Find small dabs of muddy castings among the blades of grass in a lawn.

👁 Look on the ground for holes that might have been made by poking a pencil into the earth.

👁 Look in mud puddles for wiggly lines. These trails are made by this crawling animal.

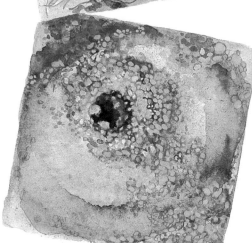

👁 Look for a small mound of sand grains with a hole in the center.

👁 Look for long lines of insects bringing food to the nest.

👁 If you look closely, you may see paths worn by these insects as they gather food.

Robin

We know spring has arrived when we hear the robin's cheerful song in our neighborhood. This gray-backed bird with orange breast feathers looks for worms in open spaces. It collects dry grass to build its cup-shaped nest. A robin's eggs are blue. Young robins crack open the blue shells as they hatch.

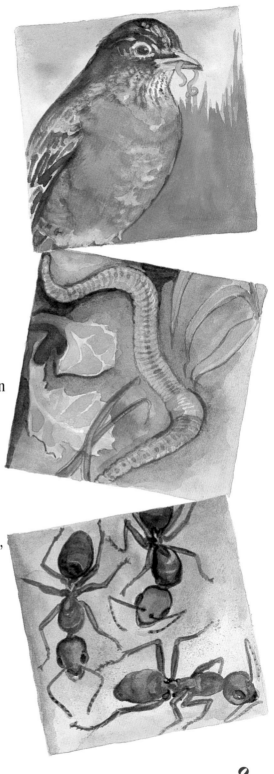

Earthworm

The earthworm's dark brown body has many segments. A fat, light-colored saddle band circles the body a short distance from the head. Earthworms dig holes through healthy soil. Soil is taken in at the worm's head as it digs. Undigested soil is cast out the rear of the worm. The castings enrich the soil.

Ant

When the spring sun warms the ground, these insects go to work on their underground nests. The ants make new rooms and care for eggs and young insects. A group of adult workers, eggs, and young larvae is called a colony.

SPRING clues

👁 Look for tracks: five toe prints, often appearing as four oval pads and a half-moon shape.

✋ Watch for soil that has been dug up and plant roots that have been thrown aside by this animal.

👃 Learn to recognize the strong smell of this animal's musk.

👁 Look for pea-sized, round brown droppings.

👁 Look for tracks with four toe prints in muddy areas under bushes and in tall grasses.

✋ Find bits of fur from this animal that it left as it brushed past low bushes.

Who has been eating plants in your environment?

Follow the trail. Find the plant, the droppings, and the animal that left the clues.

Missing seeds

Nibbled leaf

Splash of guano

Skunk

When a skunk is upset or frightened, it can spray a very nasty-smelling musk, which can travel as far as 16 feet. This mammal, which often lives near pastures and fields, is most active at night. Skunks spend a great deal of time digging in the topsoil for grubs, hornets, bumblebees, and other insects that live underground.

Cottontail Rabbit

Cottontails are mammals that eat grasses, tree bark, and leaves. Rabbits make their homes in tall grasses and bushes, which hide them from predators. Warren homes are made up of a network of passages and resting spots through the brush and grass cover. Underground tunnels are common. Rabbits have good eyesight, hearing, and sense of smell.

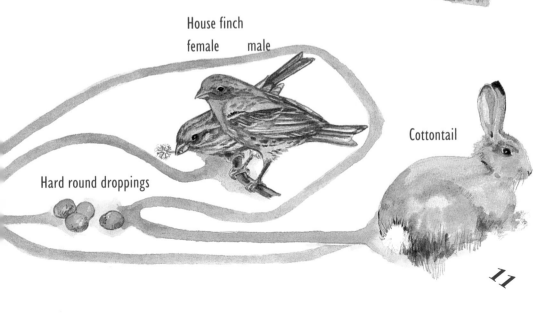

House finch
female   male

Cottontail

Hard round droppings

11

clues

👁 Look for coin-sized pits in dry sand. These small pits are shaped like cones.

✋ Find ant exoskeletons at the edge of the cone-shaped pits. The body fluids have been sucked out.

👁 Check the tops of trees for a web tent built in the branches.

👁 Look for small round droppings below trees that have web nests and damaged leaves.

Are these the same animal?

Growth stages of a mammal   Growth stages of a bird

Newborn deer   Yearling deer   Robin's egg   Robin hatchling

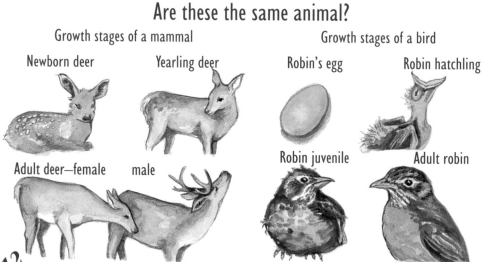

Adult deer—female   male   Robin juvenile   Adult robin

Ant Lion

The young stage (larva) of this insect creates a pit trap to catch ants. The ant lion waits buried at the bottom of the pit. It uses its large jaws to capture ants that fall into its trap. The ant lion feeds on its victim by sucking the body fluids out. Adult ant lions resemble small, brownish-gray dragonflies.

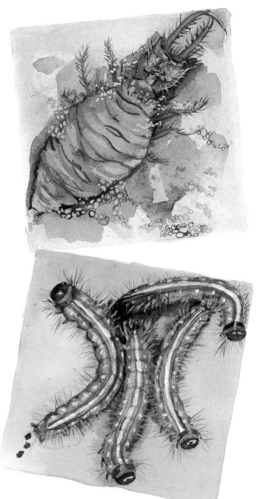

Tent Caterpillar

In spring, tent caterpillar eggs, which were laid in the fall by the adult female moth, hatch into caterpillars. These caterpillars, the larval stage of a moth, feed on leaves. Groups of them build communal web nests in the forks of tree branches. The caterpillars in a nest usually add sheets of caterpillar silk to the tent in the morning and in the evening.

As animals grow, their appearance changes.

Metamorphosis of an insect	Metamorphosis of an amphibian

Tent caterpillar egg mass   Tent caterpillar larva   Frog eggs   Maturing frog larva

Tent caterpillar pupa   Adult moth   Maturing larva Adult frog

13

clues

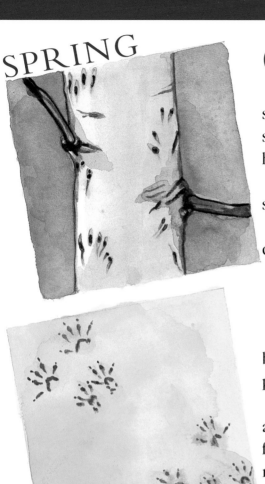

☞ Search tree trunks for claw marks showing four or five claws. This animal stands on its hind legs and reaches up as high as it can.

☞ Look for tracks that are two to seven inches long with five arching toes.

☞ Watch for large droppings that contain spring plant material.

☞ You may see these small rodents begging for food. They lose their fear of people after continuously being fed.

☞ Look for signs of seed gathering and tracks—four small toes on the front print and five bigger ones on the rear print.

℃ Listen for chattering and scolding.

☞ Watch for feeding and nest-building platforms of cattails and grasses floating in bodies of water.

☞ Check for tail drag marks that appear first on one side of the tracks and then on the other. Rear prints show webbed feet.

☌ This animal's name comes from the oily, musk-smelling secretion that males spread to mark their territory.

Black Bear

Black bears are large mammals. Their fine, kinky hair is not always black; it can be shades of brown. They hibernate in the winter in dens and emerge in the spring. Bears are very hungry after a winter of hibernation. They are omnivorous, which means they eat almost anything. They prefer budding twigs, berries, insects, and small mammals, such as squirrels.

Chipmunk

Chattering and playful behavior are characteristics of this small rodent. You see chipmunks with their cheek pouches puffed out with seeds as they head for their underground storage burrows. They are active in the daylight near piles of rocks.

Muskrat

The muskrat burrows its home in a riverbank or builds a lodge of cattails in a pond. It eats frogs, crayfish, and plants, which it finds underwater or at the water's edge. At home in wetlands and waterways, this small mammal grows to about the size of a basketball. Waterproof gray fur and a flat-sided, furless tail help make it a great swimmer.

clues

👁 Watch for distinctive K-shaped tracks, about an inch long.

👁 Look for finger-deep holes in red ant hills. These holes are often found in cracks and along the edge of sidewalks.

✋ Find long feathers with orange or red middle shafts.

🎵 Listen for loud drumming or the cry *flicka, flicka.*

👁 Look on plants for specks of white droppings called guano, left by this insect as it waits for its prey.

✋ Find a bit of silk cocoon left by this insect where it has spent the night on a plant leaf.

👁 Watch for tiny double lines of tracks in dust or sand.

👁 Look for this crustacean under rocks and leaf piles.

✋ Find an old chalk-colored exoskeleton rolled into a ball.

Flicker

The flicker, a large woodpecker, can be seen and heard drumming on trees. It nests in a hole inside a tree trunk. It is often seen on lawns or feeding along sidewalks. Flickers use their long, thick bills to probe for ants. Red ants are a flicker's favorite food.

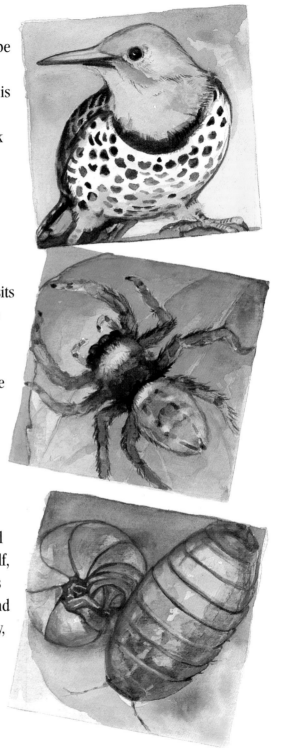

Jumping Spider

The black-and-white jumping spider sits on a plant, watching for insects with its eight sharp eyes. Its hairy body and jumping skill make this spider hard to miss. The jumping spider doesn't weave a web but spins a silk cocoon to sleep in. When an insect approaches, the spider will jump—often a distance of 20 times its length—to capture it.

Wood Louse

Often called a roly-poly because it will roll into a pea-sized ball to protect itself, the wood louse is a crustacean that has adapted to land. It eats rotting wood and plants. To protect its soft boneless body, it has a hard shell that is divided into armored sections. The shell is an exoskeleton.

SPRING

clues

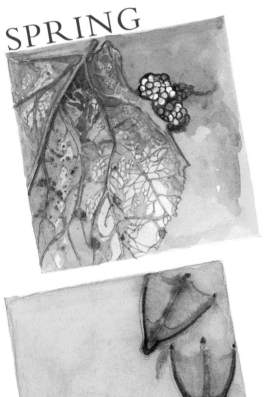

👁 In the morning, look for clear, shiny slime trails along the ground and on plants.

✋ Look closely at plant stems to see the small line that these animals make; the line becomes a scar as the plant grows.

👁 Find small, round white eggs, each smaller than a piece of rice, among brown leaves on the ground.

👁 Look for webbed tracks with three marks showing claws.

✋ Find shiny metallic-colored feathers near water.

👂 Listen for the loud quacking of the female.

Which animals are at home in these shelters?

Flicker:
nest hole builder

Nuthatch:
nest hole recycler

Snail:
shell builder

Caddis Fly:
shell recycler

Slug

Slugs are slimy, fingertip-sized animals that move by contracting their body muscle. Unlike snails, they have no shells to protect their soft brown bodies. They feed on plants and leaves that have fallen on the ground.

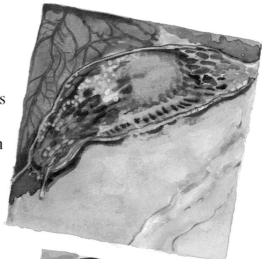

Mallard Duck

The mallard is a very common duck. The female's feathers are shades of brown; her bill is orange. The head feathers of a male mallard are iridescent green. The white neck ring, brown chest, and curl at the end of the black tail feathers are very striking. The male's bill is paler than the female's. Mallards need water and land in their habitat.

Animals are shelter builders and recyclers.

| Muskrat: lodge builder | Mallard: lodge recycler | Badger: den builder | Rabbit: den recycler |

Pretending that her wing is injured,
a startled killdeer runs from her
nest among the beach pebbles. This
act is an attempt to protect her
eggs from a predator.

in the summer

In the summer,
when there is plenty of food,
animals spend much of their time
eating and caring for and feeding their
young. Some establish territories in
which they make their homes and hunt for food.

clues

👁 Look for a very loosely built nest in a tree, a shrub, or on the ground. The nest is often built low enough so you can see if two white eggs are inside.

✋ Find pieces of white eggshells on the ground.

👂 Listen for the soft *coo-ooo, coo, coo* of the male.

👁 Look for web-footed tracks on mud banks.

👁 Look for 2-inch to 5-inch groups of jelly-like eggs floating among the water plants in clear pools.

👂 Listen for a long snort followed by a series of croaks.

Listen! What is that sound?

On summer mornings, wake up and listen. Animals are already busy. Can you hear the animal sounds outside? What do you hear? Try to figure out who makes the sounds. The sounds of buzzing might be a fly,   a bee,   or a hornet.   A cooing sound could be a mourning dove   or a pigeon. Chattering might be a tree squirrel.   The sound of drumming could be a flicker's signal.

Mourning Dove

This brown-gray bird with a pointed tail lives comfortably in many habitats—on farms, in towns, in the woods, and even in the desert. It has a very small head and large eyes. Its coo is a lovely morning sound.

Leopard Frog

Look for the leopard frog in and near ponds and other shallow bodies of water with water plants rooted in them. Leopard frogs are amphibians that can live in water and on land. After hatching from soft eggs as tadpoles, they slowly grow legs and lose their tails as they mature into frogs. This frog is well camouflaged by its green color and black spots.

Animal sounds are all around us. Listen!

On summer evenings, sit in a yard or park. As the sky darkens, listen to the animal sounds. You will hear the sounds of insects and other animals calling in a summer choir. The sound of creaking could be a frog. Buzzing may tell you a mosquito is about to make a meal of your blood. A chirping sound could be made by a cricket or a bird. Barking and howling may come from a dog or its wild relative—a coyote.

clues

👁 Look along the water's edge for a short dirt column made of dabs of mud.

✋ As you walk along the water's edge, look for an exoskeleton that this animal has outgrown and discarded.

👁 Look for the exoskeleton of the nymph attached about 3 feet up on a tree trunk.

👂 Listen for the loud buzz of the adult male insect coming from the top of the trees.

Bones inside or outside?

Some animals have skeletons and some have exoskeletons.
Bones on the inside: The animal has a skeleton, which grows along with the growing animal.

Bobcat: a mammal   Frog: a reptile   Crow: a bird

Crayfish

Crayfish are crustaceans that live in fresh water and look like small lobsters. This animal's exoskeleton has sections that protect it from predators. Crayfish burrow into the mud for shelter, leaving a column of mud above their burrow. Insects and small fish become food for a crayfish, which creeps along the river bottom at night.

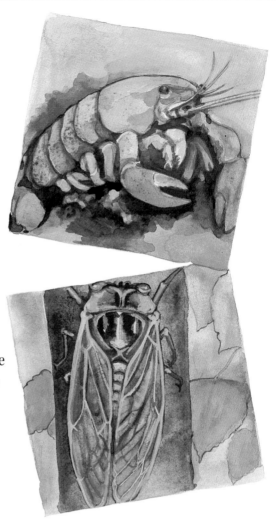

Cicada

In late summer we hear this insect's buzzing call to its mate. The cicada lays eggs in a twig at the treetop. In the fall the twig drops to the ground. Cicada nymphs burrow underground and eat tree roots for as long as two years. Then the larvae come out of the soil and crawl up a tree. They push out of their exoskeletons through a star slit on their back.

Bones on the outside: The animal has an exoskeleton, which may be outgrown and discarded.

Orb weaver: a spider   Cicada: an insect   Crayfish: a crustacean

25

clues

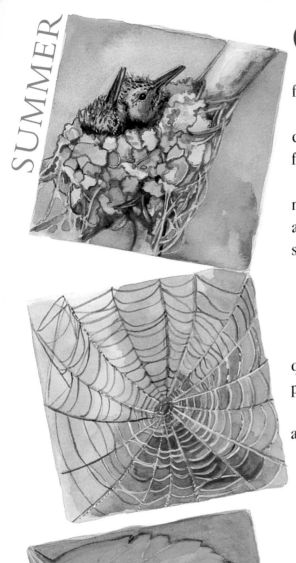

℃ Listen for the hum of this bird's fast-moving wings.

℃ Listen for the buzzing and chirping calls as the birds defend their mates and feeding places.

👁 Look for very small, well-insulated nests made of lichen, soft plant materials, and spider webs. The cup-shaped, palm-sized nests are often hidden in bushes.

👁 Look for a large circular web.

👁 In early spring look for round, quarter-sized egg sacs on the stems of plants. The sacs are full of baby spiders.

✋ Find old exoskeletons of this animal clinging to plants.

✋ Look for moon-shaped cuts in small leaves and flower petals.

℃ Listen for the soft buzz of this busy small insect.

Hummingbird

Hummingbirds hover as they sip nectar from flowers. Moving their wings to stay suspended in air, they can maneuver up, down, and backward as they feed. The bird inserts its long sipping bill into flowers to get the nectar. The hum we hear comes from the rapid movement of their wings. Hummingbirds are attracted to red flowers.

Orb Weaver Spider

People like having orb weaver spiders in their gardens because they eat lots of plant-eating insects and help protect the garden plants. Like all spiders, they have eight legs. The exoskeletons are shed as the spiders grow.

Leafcutter Bee

The female leafcutter bee uses a hole in rotted wood or between bricks or in the ground to lay her eggs. The bee lines the hole with a piece of leaf or flower petal that she has cut. She fills the leaf with flower pollen and nectar for her young. Then she lays her eggs on top and seals the hole with another leaf piece.

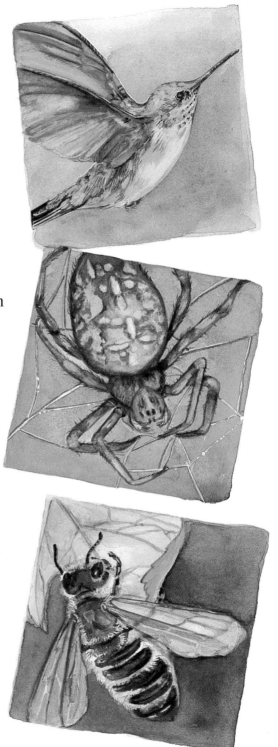

clues

👁 Look for very large piles of droppings. Dung mounds can be seen from a safe distance across a field.

👁 Look for large, deep hoof tracks made by a very large animal that can weigh as much as 2,000 pounds.

𝄐 Listen, from a distance, for loud snorts, roars, and stomping.

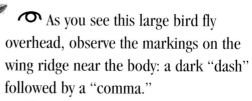

👁 As you see this large bird fly overhead, observe the markings on the wing ridge near the body: a dark "dash" followed by a "comma."

👁 Watch for nests of sticks in woods near open meadows.

✋ Look for large brown or rust-colored feathers.

𝄐 Listen for a loud screech.

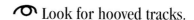

👁 Look for hooved tracks.

𝄐 Listen for the sound of an animal blowing out air.

👁 Look for cylinder-shaped, dark brown droppings.

VISIT THE HABITAT OF THESE ANIMALS

OUR NATIONAL PARKS • FORESTS • PRESERVES • WILDERNESS AREAS

Bison

Herds of bison eat large amounts of grasses. Their large droppings, which contain undigested seeds and digested plant material, fertilize their habitat, replanting the seeds of the grasses they eat. Bison are endangered. Once there were millions. Today only about a thousand range free. But domestic herds are raised in many states.

Red-tailed Hawk

Perched along roadsides on posts and poles, this large hawk waits patiently to spot its food—a rodent or a small animal—on the ground. You may also observe this bird of prey soaring gracefully in the air over open fields.

Pronghorn

Pronghorns are among the world's fastest animals. They live on the prairies and grasslands of western North America. Males and females both have horns with two points called prongs. Pronghorn herds travel to the areas where grasses and shrubs are most nutritious.

clues

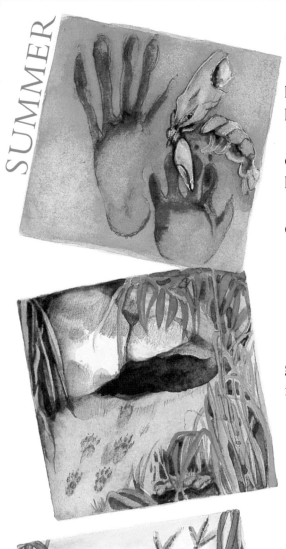

👁 Look for tracks near water. Both hind and front prints resemble human hands, but the hind tracks are larger.

✋ Look for crayfish shell bits left on rocks where these animals may have eaten.

👁 Observe black, rope-like droppings on the top of a rock.

👁 Look for tracks in the sand.

👁 Watch for small trails through the grass that end at the entrance hole to this rodent's underground burrow.

👁 Look for three-pronged tracks in the sand.

✋ Watch for gray-brown feathers.

𝐂 Listen for the bird to repeat its name: *kill-deer.*

Raccoon

Raccoons are very intelligent animals that can use their paws to catch small animals and to pick nuts and fruits. They wash or wet their food before eating. Raccoons are mammals found in areas with water and good den sites, such as caves, underground burrows, or piles of brush. They are nocturnal—often awake and active at night.

Thirteen-lined Ground Squirrel

You might see this rodent in dry tall-grass areas. The 13 lines help camouflage this squirrel as it stands in the grass eating seeds. The lines are a pattern of dark and light brown patches of fur. The ground squirrel hibernates in winter.

Killdeer

This brown shorebird with two black breast bands lives at the water's edge and lays its eggs among beach pebbles. The speckled eggs look like the surrounding pebbles and dirt. The killdeer may lead you away from its nest by pretending to have a broken wing.

clues

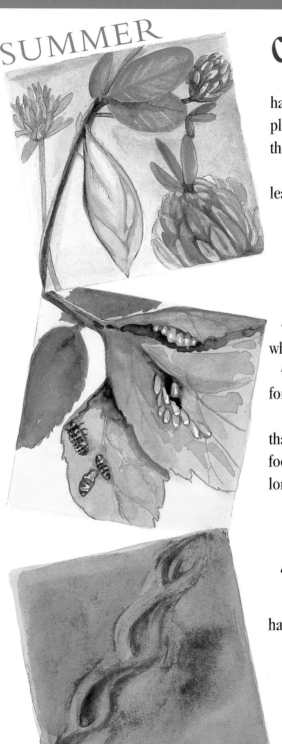

✋ Look in meadows for shrubs that have leaves with holes. Search these plants for smooth green caterpillars—the larval stage of this insect.

✋ Look for cocoons attached to plant leaves and stems with silk threads.

👁 Look for this beetle on plants where sticky aphids are present.

👁 Look on the underside of leaves for many tiny yellow eggs.

✋ Observe clusters of exoskeletons that indicate these beetles may have been food for a predator such as a daddy longlegs spider.

👁 Look for long coiling tracks.

✋ Find the skin that this reptile has shed.

Sulphur Butterfly

This familiar insect, which has shades of yellow and white (like butter), was the first to be named "butterfly." It can be seen fluttering across sunny fields in large numbers. Sulphur butterflies have full-sized front legs and often walk around mud puddles in large groups.

Ladybug

The ladybug is a small spotted beetle that is familiar to most of us. Ladybugs eat aphids that damage garden and lawn plants. This beetle, with its black spots and red wings, is sometimes found in groups. When they are frightened, some ladybugs produce a very smelly, orange substance from their front legs.

Garter Snake

A stripe of yellow, green, or orange runs from the head to the tail of this olive or brown reptile. Garter snakes live along the edges of streams and ponds and in other wetland areas. Garter snakes can be as long as 3 feet. They eat frogs, fish, earthworms, slugs, and salamanders. Garter snakes are most active on summer days.

A red fox stops at the entrance to its burrow. Disturbed by the harvesting activity, a bull snake has emerged from a field. The exposed bull snake is in danger of becoming the prey of this fox.

as the leaves dry

As the leaves dry and fruits and nuts ripen in the fall, animals are busy eating or storing large amounts of food to use during winter. Some animals compete for mates and still others begin long journeys to warm climates.

35

clues

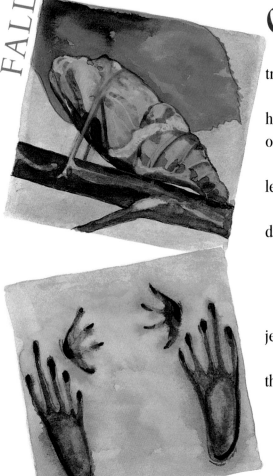

👁 Look for cocoons that hang below tree branches or plant leaves.

🐛 The larva that grows into this insect has a scent organ on its head that gives off a foul-smelling substance.

👁 Look for larvae curled inside leaves as they eat.

👁 Observe small, black oval droppings below chewed leaves.

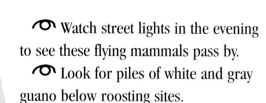

👁 Look for large floating masses of jelly-like eggs.

🎵 Listen for the *m-rum* rumble of the male's calls.

👁 Watch street lights in the evening to see these flying mammals pass by.

👁 Look for piles of white and gray guano below roosting sites.

Tiger Swallowtail Butterfly

The black and yellow tiger swallowtail butterfly has a long tail at the base of each wing. It often has red and blue spots. All butterflies begin life as caterpillars. When the caterpillar is ready for the pupal stage of its life, it forms a cocoon from which the butterfly emerges.

Bullfrog

Bullfrogs are always close to water. They particularly like ponds with many water plants. This green frog will eat any animal it can swallow—including other frogs and even other bullfrogs! A female bullfrog can lay 20,000 jelly-like eggs in the water. The eggs hatch into tadpoles in a few days. The tadpoles mature into adults that can be 7 inches long.

Little Brown Bat

Little brown bats often use buildings as roosting sites. This bat is the size of a small hand. People benefit from bats because each bat can eat about 8 insects a minute. A bat can fill its stomach in 15 minutes and empty its digestive system many times in one night—that means a lot fewer mosquitoes.

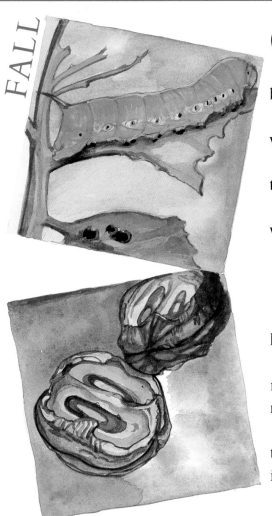

clues

👁 Look for these flying insects resting below porch lights in the day.

👁 Look for the very large green larva with a large horn-like point at its tail end.

✋ Look for plants that are missing their upper leaves.

👁 Look below tomato plants or grape vines for dark, eraser-sized droppings.

👁 Look for nests made of dry leaves high in trees.

✋ Find the shells of nuts. These rodents chew open the nuts to eat the soft meat inside.

👂 Listen to these rodents chatter as they let other animals know of intruders in their territory.

Examine the clues you find!

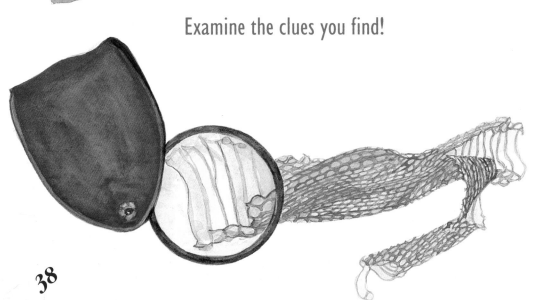

Sphinx Moth

The sphinx moth is sometimes mistaken for a hummingbird because its wings move very quickly as it sips nectar from flowers. This insect lives near gardens and crop fields. The big, green tomato hornworm is the caterpillar stage of one of the many species of sphinx moths.

Fox Squirrel

Fox squirrels do very well in cities and suburbs with a variety of trees. They make nests high in the trees for the winter. In warmer weather they may make several lower nests. Fall is spent eating and burying nuts for winter. Each squirrel hides its cache of nuts, burying each nut individually.

Old fur, feathers, and skin tell you which animals are around.

Animal coats of feathers, fur, and skin are always being replaced. The old feathers, bits of fur, and skin that are shed are wonderful evidence clues because they can be collected and examined.

clues

🖐 Look for the shed skin of this reptile. It is like transparent paper ribbon and is tube shaped.

👁 Look for long S-shaped tracks.

👂 Listen for a hiss and the sound of a vibrating tail in leaves or grass.

👁 Look for a group of these large birds in flight in a V-shaped formation.

👂 Listen for loud honks as these birds fly overhead.

👁 Watch for many web-footed tracks in grain fields. Long rounded droppings are usually present, too.

👁 Look for horizontal drill holes in tree trunks.

👂 Listen for a slow *wheeer* call and the sound of the bird drilling into a trunk to get to the tree's sap.

Bull Snake

This reptile is often killed because it makes a sound like a rattlesnake when it is frightened. Many farmers and ranchers are happy to have bull snakes around because they eat mice and rats. As the weather cools, bull snakes may move to exposed places to warm their cold-blooded bodies in the sun.

Canada Goose

The sight of geese flying south lets us know winter is on the way. The migrating geese stop at ponds and grain fields along the way. These stopover spots are very important to geese because they need to rest and eat for the next part of their journey. The geese store up fat to provide "fuel" for their flight.

Yellow-bellied Sapsucker

A sapsucker is a woodpecker that gets its name because it likes to suck the sap of trees. It drills orderly rows of horizontal holes in the tree. The birds nest in holes drilled down into the tree trunk. The sapsucker has a slight crest of feathers on its head.

clues

👁 In some areas, observation spots are set up at a distance from the nests of these raptors to avoid disturbing them. From the observation area you can look through binoculars and see the birds at their nest.

✋ Large oval pellets containing rabbit bones and fur may have been thrown up by this large raptor.

👁 Look for bent and broken branches on young trees that indicate these large mammals were rubbing their antlers against the branches.

👁 Look for large tracks and large areas of flattened grass or snow where a herd has slept.

👂 Listen for the bugling of the male in the fall.

👁 Look for tracks of five toes along mud banks near the lodges built by these mammals. Hind prints are larger than front ones and are webbed.

✋ Look for wood chips about 1 to 2 inches in length near tree stumps.

👂 Listen for the sound of a tail slap in the water as a warning that you, an intruder, are nearby.

Golden Eagle

This bird of prey stands over 3 feet tall. With "eagle eyes" it can spot prey, most often a rabbit, from a great distance. The eagle's long powerful wings allow it to swoop down and capture its prey with large claws called talons. Eagles often return to the same nests each year. They prefer sites that are far from people.

Elk

The large mammal we call an elk is often called a wapiti by Native Americans. In the fall, the bulls come out of the woods and use loud bugling calls to attract female elk. The most vocal elk attracts the greatest number of mates. Female elk and their young travel in herds. Bull elk have antlers that can weigh as much as 30 pounds.

Beaver

The beaver, a mammal, cuts down small trees with its strong teeth. It then uses the twigs and logs to build its well-engineered dams and lodges in the water. It eats willow bark and twigs. Look for beavers in the evening.

OUR NATIONAL PARKS · FORESTS · WILDERNESS AREAS · PRESERVES

VISIT THE HABITAT OF THESE ANIMALS

clues

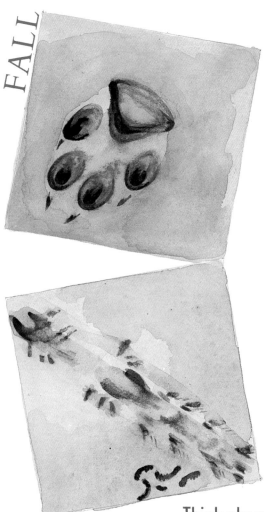

🐾 Watch for droppings that are thin and as long as 4 inches. You can often see hairs in the droppings.

🐾 Look for oval-shaped tracks.

🦻 Listen for yipping and barking.

🐾 Look for holes in leaves where an insect has dined.

🐾 Look for droppings on leaves below the ones that have been eaten.

🦻 Listen for the trilling song: *katy-did-katy-didn't.*

Think about the features of an animal's tracks.

I. Check the size, shape, and depth of the print.

Size

Shape

2. Does the animal have claws, hooves, pads, or toes? Do claws and toes show?

Claws

Hooves

Pads/toes

Red Fox

Foxes are very playful within their families. They live in many places, including business parks and suburbs where they can find a good den and mice and voles to eat. This mammal is the size of a small dog. The body of the animal is red, silver, and sometimes black. The fox has black legs and ear tips. Foxes often raise their young in underground dens dug by other animals.

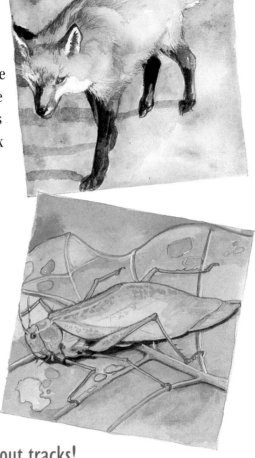

Katydid

Many animals blend into their surroundings. A katydid is an insect that is well camouflaged because it is green and looks like the green leaves of the plants it eats. The katydid's strong rear grasshopper-type legs enable it to hop. Katydids can also fly.

Checking out tracks!

3. Do the tracks show

two feet,   four feet,

or more than four feet?

4. How do the hind tracks differ from the front ones? Rear tracks are usually bigger than the front ones. Does the size or shape differ?

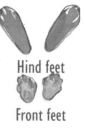

Hind feet

Front feet

5. Is there a drag mark from a tail?

clues

☞ Look for tracks with "thumbs" that are spaced far from the toes.

☞ A very stinky smell may come from this animal when it is trying to discourage a predator.

☞ Listen for clicking sounds or angry growls and squeals.

✋ Look for empty spiral-shaped shells. Some may have been cracked by birds that eat these mollusks.

✋ Look for plants that are scarred with small lines by this animal's tooth.

Who left that shiny little trail of slime?

A slime trail is shiny and transparent. Most trails are observed on the ground. These trails consist of mucous, which is produced by snails and slugs under certain conditions, particularly when they are attacked by a predator. The slime has a strong offensive smell. Females lay tiny, bead-like white eggs that are protected by a layer of slime. During the winter, snails seal their shell openings with a plug of slime that hardens and keeps in moisture.

Opossum

This marsupial mammal, which will eat anything, lives in woodlands that have flowing streams. The opossum carries its babies in a belly pouch. When an opossum is threatened by a predator, it curls up and lies still. We call this "playing possum."

Snail

Snails are mollusks that live in moist places such as woodlands and gardens. The shell that protects a snail's soft body spirals as it grows and provides a protective home, which the snail carries on its back. The snail eats plant tissue, which it scrapes off with its tooth.

Be a slime sleuth!

When you see a shiny trail of slime on the ground, you may be able to determine what left the trail. Put a board on the ground overnight. In the morning lift the board. Small animals like snails, slugs, wood lice, worms, and centipedes will hide under the board. Most of these creatures are using the board to hide from predators and escape from the sun's heat. The centipede, however, is a very aggressive hunter and preys on any animal of a similar size.

A long-tailed weasel has left a distinctive trail of
diving and jumping holes in the snow.
A meadow vole burrows along under the snow as it
searches for insects to eat .
The long-tailed weasel searches for voles.

cold weather

Cold weather makes many animals slow down. Some hibernate. Others work hard to stay warm and find food. The clues to their presence are all around. The snow that covers the ground provides signs of animals.

clues

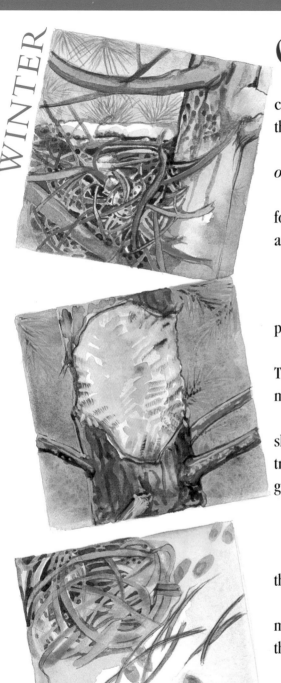

✋ Look on the ground for pellets that contain bits of bones, fur, or feathers of the animals that this bird has eaten.

☾ Listen at night for this bird's call: *oho, hoo-hoo-hoo, hoo.*

👁 Check open snow-covered areas for the print of this raptor's wings made as it swooped down to capture a mouse.

👁 Look for tracks with toes that point in.

👁 Look for chewed bark on trees. Trees may have a high ring of bark missing from their trunk.

✋ Find pointed quills with hollow shafts. Trails and roads near "ringed" trees are a good place to check the ground for quills.

☾ In quiet meadows you can hear these animals moving under the snow.

👁 Look across a snow-covered meadow for small holes through which these animals surface and dive.

👁 Trails made by other animals may be used as runways by this rodent. Look for small, black oval droppings. You may even spot one of these animals running along the trails.

Great Horned Owl

This large owl hunts rabbits, mice, voles, and small birds. Owls are most active at night. Because it can swivel its head almost completely around, the owl can see to the sides and behind it. Owls live anywhere they find plenty of food.

Porcupine

The porcupine, a good tree climber, eats leaves, bark, and twigs. It defends itself by using a muscle in its skin to make the quills on its back and tail stand erect. Erect quills easily come loose from the porcupine's skin. An attacker who touches the quills or is hit by the porcupine's tail is speared by the quills' sharp tips.

Vole

In the winter, meadows are great places to find evidence of voles. Voles are rodents about the size of a small hand. Their heads are larger than those of mice and they have short tails. Voles eat large quantities of food, including seeds, grains, bark, fruits, insects, snails, and worms.

OUR NATIONAL PARKS · FORESTS ·
VISIT
THE HABITAT
OF THESE
ANIMALS
WILDERNESS AREAS · PRESERVES ·

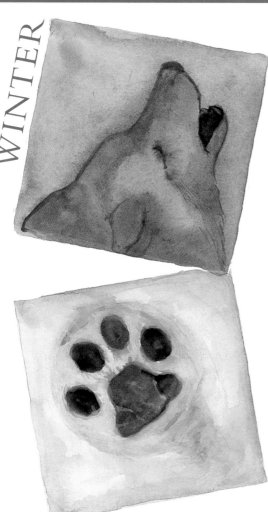

clues

👁 Watch for territory markers that consist of urine and droppings.

👁 Look for tracks going across open fields. The claw marks will be visible.

𝒞 Listen for dog-like howls.

OUR NATIONAL PARKS · FORESTS · VISIT THE HABITAT OF THESE ANIMALS · WILDERNESS AREAS · PRESERVES

👁 Look for round tracks in sets of four. These tracks show this animal's four toe pads.

👁 Watch for droppings that look like those of a house cat but are larger.

👁 Watch for droppings that are not covered by dirt.

Who has been preying on the animals in your environment?

Find tracks and trails. Check for pellets and droppings.
Find the animal that left the clues.

Imprint of wings in snow

Tracks with five toes

Tracks

Pellet

Coyote

The coyote is a canine—a dog-like animal. Coyotes are often spotted as they hunt mice and other animals in open fields. Among their few predators are humans. Coyotes, like dogs, urinate on trees to mark their territory. Their droppings look like those of a dog. But unlike dogs, coyotes spread around their droppings, probably as additional markers.

Bobcat

Bobcats eat birds and small mammals such as rabbits. They occasionally eat large animals. Like most cats, bobcats are nocturnal and territorial. The bobcat will cover its droppings when it hunts outside its territory. Uncovered droppings that are spread out and scratched indicate the bobcat is in its territory.

Long-tailed weasel

Tracks
with three toes

Droppings

Great horned owl

53

clues

✋ Look for large blue-black feathers.

👁 Observe bowl-like nests made of sticks and lined with soft materials.

👁 Find pellets that contain plant and animal remains. Insect parts and berry seeds are examples of the material you might see in this bird's pellets.

𝒞 Listen for the *caw-caw* danger cry.

👁 Look for nests that have been made low in bushes or shrubs. These nests are cup-shaped and built very loosely of small sticks and grasses.

✋ Look for red feathers that have been shed by the male.

𝒞 Listen for the call: a sharp *chink*.

👁 Look for small tracks in dust.

👁 Watch for tiny, oval black droppings and small chew marks on food containers, such as bags of flour.

𝒞 Listen for soft scratching sounds.

Crow

A black-feathered and thick-billed bird, the crow is so adaptable that it can live in almost any habitat that has trees. Crows often nest in large groups. Their greenish, spotted eggs are usually laid in groups of four to six in bowl-shaped nests. Crows will eat almost anything, particularly the remains of animals that have been killed on the road.

Cardinal

It is hard to miss the bright red coat and crested head of the male cardinal. Females have more brown feathers on their chests and backs than the males. Cardinals do not migrate when the weather grows cold and snow falls. This bird can often be seen feeding on the ground or at bird feeders. It lives in bushy areas.

Mouse

In cold weather, mice often seek shelter in buildings. They build tight warm nests of available material. Mice are small mammals that have short lives, but they produce many young. These animals are secretive creatures that hunt at night for insects and seeds.

clues

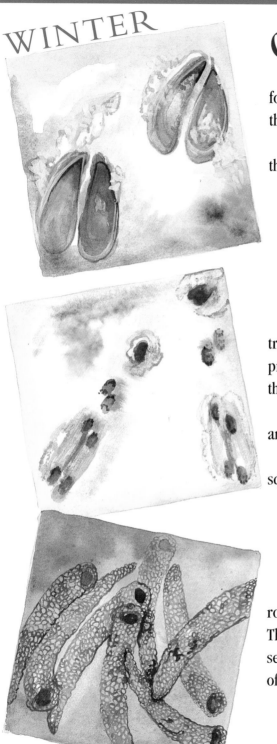

👁 Look for heart-shaped tracks and for oval pellet droppings that are about the size of a nickel.

👁 Look for territory marks: trees that the male has rubbed with its antlers.

𝓒 Listen for snorting alarm signals.

👁 Look for tracks in the snow. The tracks are connected to the next set of prints by a drag line. Tracks stop when these animals dive below the snow.

𝓒 Listen for warning foot-stomping and clicking sounds.

𝓒 These animals may whistle or squeal and hiss as they hunt.

👁 Look for larva cases attached to rocks in ponds and flowing streams. These cylinder-shaped casings are easy to see in winter because the water is clear of plants.

White-tailed Deer

When startled, these deer lift their white tail "flag" as they bound away. In the winter male deer have antlers but the females do not. These deer live in woodlands and agricultural areas that have good sources of water. In the winter, small herds of white-tailed deer seek areas that provide shelter and food.

Long-tailed Weasel

The large, long-tailed weasel springs along with its back arched. In winter, its brown fur turns white except for the black tip on the tail. Weasels live in dens in the ground, under fallen trees, or among rocks. They bury food, such as mice and voles, near their dens.

Caddis Fly

In its larval stage, this insect is found in streams and ponds. The larva, which looks a bit like a caterpillar, spins a tube of silk, attaching to it material such as bits of sand and plants. When the brown-winged adult is ready to mature, it breaks open its cocoon and flies away, leaving its underwater home.

clues

✋ Find nibbled leaves and branches on shrubs.

👁 Watch for round pellet scat slightly bigger than a pea.

👁 Look for hopping tracks in the snow. Small front prints are set behind large hind foot prints. The large prints are side by side.

✋ Find black-banded tail feathers.

👁 Look below niche-nesting spots for pellets that contain rodent bones and fur.

𝐂 Listen for the loud cry: *killy-killy.*

👁 Watch for these colorful birds on telephone poles and wires. The males have light blue wings; the females have red-brown wings.

✋ Find an exoskeleton that an adult has molted and left behind.

👁 Watch for small, round black droppings, about the size of a period.

✋ Look for parts of dead insects—the large, chicken-like back legs, for example.

𝐂 Listen for a high-pitched chirp that is made by the male as it rubs its legs to attract a female.

Jackrabbit

In the winter a jackrabbit, which is usually brown, has a light coat. In some locations, it is white. Its winter food is mainly shrubs. Jackrabbits use their great speed to escape predators like coyotes, eagles, and humans. As an additional defense against predators, jackrabbits are nocturnal; the darkness helps them hide.

Kestrel

This raptor is a bird of prey that eats small rodents and grasshoppers. It lives where food is plentiful—often in towns and cities. Kestrels can be seen perching on poles, posts, and wires along roads. They often find shelter in the niches of buildings. Kestrels are the smallest falcons. They are about 1 foot long.

Cricket

In the fall, many crickets that live outdoors join crickets that live in our homes all year long. House crickets eat crumbs of food. The outdoor crickets eat seeds, plants, and dead insects. This brown insect can grow to 1 inch in length. Its exoskeleton looks like a cricket but it is light-colored and hollow.

Trailing a story!

Track trails can be confusing, but it is fun to try to figure them out! They often tell you a story. Ask yourself these questions when you see animal trails.

What was the animal's size and at what speed was it traveling?

Was the track made by a big animal moving quickly by pushing hard off the ground or was it a small animal moving softly, slowly? Consider the size of the track. Note how deeply the track is pressed into the ground or snow. How much ground is covered by one set of prints? These clues indicate the size of the animal. What is the distance between the set of prints? This distance indicates the speed of the animal. A greater distance between sets of prints would indicate the animal was moving quickly—running, bounding, or hopping. A shorter distance shows the animal was walking.

In what direction was the animal traveling?

Which way do the toes or hooves seem to

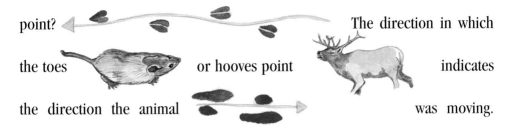

point? The direction in which the toes or hooves point indicates the direction the animal was moving.

What other clues indicate more about the trail story?

Are there many different kinds of animal tracks? These may indicate animals were hunting or that a good trail was used by many animals. Similar tracks may be from a group or from one animal using the same trail many times. Are there clues to eating, drinking, or sleeping? Look for signs of eating or drinking. To find out whose trail you are on, it is helpful to observe droppings and pellets. Round or cylinder-shaped droppings are usually from plant-eating animals. Long coiling droppings are often from animals that eat other animals. Pellets are oval balls of bone and fur that are thrown up by birds of prey. Packed-down grass or snow shows a spot where animals rested.

GLOSSARY

Amphibians: Cold-blooded animals with backbones. Many live on both land and water; most lay their eggs in water. Examples: frog, toad, newt.

Burrow: A tunnel or hole that animals make to create a home for their young.

Call: A sound that an animal makes to warn possible enemies or to communicate with a mate.

Castings: Animals, such as earthworms, leave these tiny mountains made of mud bits.

Crustaceans: Animals with a hard outer shell and no backbone that live mainly in the water. Examples: crabs, shrimp, lobsters. The roly-poly (or wood louse) is an example of a crustacean that lives on land.

Cry: A special sound, like a call, that an animal makes which is different from that of other animals.

Den: An animal's home that it finds or sometimes makes by digging; usually protected by rock, tree roots, or plants.

Droppings: An animal's solid waste.

Ecology: The study of animals and plants as they interact with each other and their environment.

Exoskeleton: A hard covering on the outside of an animal that works like a skeleton. Examples: crayfish, spiders, and insects have exoskeletons.

Gland smells: Smells that come from internal fluid sacs; animals spray or rub the liquid to mark their territory.

Guano: The droppings of birds, insects, and some mammals, such as bats.

Habitat: A place where an animal or plant lives, such as in the mountains or in a tide pool.

Hibernation: An animal's resting state during the winter.

Larva: A young insect or other animal whose appearance changes as it develops. A caterpillar is the larva of a mature butterfly. A tadpole is the larva of a mature frog.

Mammal: A warm-blooded animal that feeds its young milk. Mammals have backbones as well as fur or hair. They also have a special kind of jointed jawbone. Examples: raccoon, puma, deer, human.

Marsupial: Female marsupials are mammals that carry their young in a pouch. Opossum are marsupials.

Metamorphosis: The process of an animal changing into a new form, such as egg to larva or nymph to adult.